She's So Social

A Guide to Building Self-Confidence, Strong Relationships, and Making Smart Choices

I am flying with a whole lot of confidence!

She's So Social

A Guide to Building Self-Confidence, Strong Relationships, and Making Smart Choices

WORKBOOK

Latoya Abdouramane

Helping Girls Navigate the World with Confidence

 An Imprint of That Generation Publishing

This book is a work of nonfiction. Any resemblance to an actual person, living or dead, or actual events is purely coincidental where noted.

That Generation Publishing books and services may be purchased for educational, business, or sales promotional use. For information, please email thatgeneration1@gmail.com.

Library of Congress Cataloging-in-Publication Data has been applied for.
ISBN: 979-8-9944416-0-2
Library of Congress Control Number: 2026906500

To all the girls who have lost confidence,
faced struggles,
and doubted their strength.

Close your eyes and make a wish!

Contents

I Pledge To:

♡ Always be me, love myself, and believe in myself

♡ Find joy in learning new things

♡ Speak kindly to myself every day

♡ Become a positive force in my family and community

♡ Make smart choices and learn from my mistakes

♡ Be the kind of friend I would love to have

♡ Never compare myself to others

♡ Laugh Out Loud every day

♡ Do my best in school

♡ Communicate with respect

♡ Learn so I can teach

♡ Have fun

♡ Remember that I am beautiful inside and out

Sign HERE: _________________________________ Date: ______________

No two flowers are the same!
ADD SOME COLOR TO ME!

Introduction

Imagine you're standing on stage in the school's gym, ready to recite your lines. Your heart is racing, and the whole school is staring at you. But as soon as you look around, you see your friend who helped you practice your lines; she's cheering you on, and you feel stronger. You take a deep breath, step forward, and shine.

This is what confidence feels like. It's not about being perfect; it's about believing in yourself and feeling good about who you are, just like when you take on that big challenge and know you've got this!

In this book, you'll explore some important topics to help you build confidence, strong relationships, and make smart choices. These include:

- **Self-Esteem**: Learning to feel proud of who you are and what you can do.
- **Decision Making**: Choosing what's right for you, even when things get tricky.
- **Peer Pressure**: Knowing how to handle those moments when others try to push you to do something you're not comfortable with.
- **Impact of Social Media**: Understanding how social media affects how you see yourself and how to use it in a healthy way.
- **Self-Control**: Learning to stay calm and make choices that help you grow.
- **Communication**: Express yourself clearly and respectfully so others can understand and respect you.

These skills will help you become more confident, make informed choices, and build strong, positive relationships with your friends, family, and those around you.

Ready to get started? **Follow Me!**

Benefits of Building Self-Confidence, Strong Relationships, and Making Smart Choices

Right now, you might be thinking that building self-confidence, having strong relationships, and making smart choices sounds hard, even too hard. You might feel like you don't have the strength yet. But don't let that little voice in your head stop you from growing into the amazing girl you're meant to be.

This book is here to help you. Inside, you'll find simple tips that make confidence easier to build, plus fun and cool exercises you can try every day. The activities will help you grow your "confidence" so you can feel stronger, braver, and sure of yourself **over time**.

As you grow stronger on the inside, you'll start to feel better about who you are. You'll notice you can do things that once felt scary or impossible, like speaking up, making good choices, or managing tricky friendship moments.

How to Use This Book

This book has **six chapters**, each of which helps you grow stronger: **Highlighting Positive Qualities, Making Smart Choices, Navigating Friendships, The Social Media World, Managing Your Emotions,** and **The Power of Words**. Inside each chapter, you'll find short sections with fun activities, real-life situations, and writing exercises to help you think, reflect, and grow. By the time you finish this book, you'll have the tools you need to be **"So Social"** in a healthy and confident way.

You don't have to read this book in order. If there's something you're struggling with right now, or something you're curious about, you can jump to that chapter first. Still, I encourage you to come back and read all the chapters eventually, because each one includes different "social" exercises that can help you in many situations.

You might be surprised to find that some chapters really connect with you, even more than you expected. And just because something isn't hard for you right now doesn't mean it won't be later. It's easy to feel confident when everything is going great, but it can be harder to see your positive qualities after a tough test or when a friendship feels different. Doing these activities ahead of time helps you be ready for those moments.

The exercises in this book aren't just for tough times; they're also for good times. Building your confidence helps you enjoy life, feel proud of yourself, and make the most out of fun moments too. Even if you think you've already mastered a skill, practicing it again can help build more confidence.

So, grab your favorite-colored gel pens, bring an open mind, and get ready to be **"So Social!"**

You are amazing Just as you are!

❀ 1 Highlighting Positive Qualities

Hey girl, hi!

You are amazing just the way you are! This chapter is all about discovering what makes you 'YOU,' your strengths, talents, and all the little things that make you unique. We'll talk about how to build confidence, kick negative thoughts to the side, and cheer yourself on! Learning to love and appreciate yourself is beautiful, and by the end of this chapter, you'll be rocking that confidence like your favorite sweatshirt! Let's go!

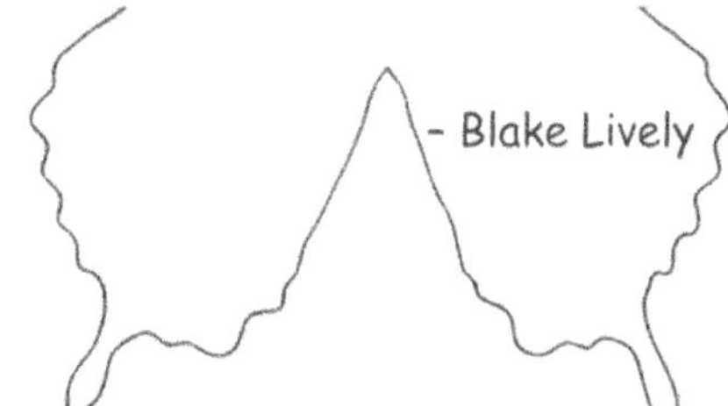

Building Self-Confidence

Self-confidence means believing in yourself and your abilities. Sometimes, it's easy to feel unsure or to compare yourself to others but remember everyone has strengths. Here are some ways to highlight your strengths and help you build your confidence:

❊ **Keep a Confidence Journal:** Write down one thing you did well each day. It could be answering a question in class, helping a friend, or cleaning your room.

↳ **Check This Out:** Olivia was nervous about presenting her poem in class, so she practiced and did her best. That evening, she wrote in her journal, "I spoke clearly and shared my writing!"

Start your journal entries on the following page…

Confidence Journal STARTS HERE!

Building Self-Confidence Continues...

❋ **Step Outside Your Comfort Zone:** Try new activities, even if they seem scary. Confidence grows when you challenge yourself.

↳ **Check This Out:** Stevie was afraid to try out for the soccer team, but she gave it a shot and made new friends in the process!

Name an activity you tried that seemed scary at first, but you are happy you stepped out of your comfort zone:

____

____

____

____

Tell me about an activity you want to try and what's holding you back.

____

____

____

____

Building Self-Confidence Continues…

❋ **Power Poses:** Sometimes your body can help your mind feel strong and ready to take on anything. Try these fun 'poses' to boost your confidence and remind yourself how amazing you are!

1. The Fire Girl Pose

- Stand tall with your feet apart like a superhero on a mission.
- Put your hands on your hips.
- Lift your chin and look straight ahead like you're about to save the day.
- Take a big, deep breath and feel your power!

☺ **Say it to yourself:** "I've got this!"

2. The Victoria Pose

- Stand tall and stretch your arms up into a big "V" shape.
- Smile big and imagine you just won something cool.
- Hold the pose for a few seconds while taking deep breaths.

☺ **Say it to yourself:** "I'm proud of me!"

3. The Model Pose

- Stand with your feet shoulder-width apart.
- Let your arms hang relaxed by your sides.
- Take up space, no slouching or crossing your arms!
- Breathe in slowly through your nose, out through your mouth.

☺ **Say it to yourself:** "I belong here."

Identifying and Challenging Negative Self-Talk

Negative self-talk happens when you tell yourself things like, "I'm not good enough," or "I can't do this." These thoughts can make you feel bad about yourself, even when they're not true.

Here's how to challenge them:

❋ **Catch that Thought:** The next time you think something negative about yourself, **stop,** and ask, "Is this true?"

⤷ **Check This Out:** Aubree thinks, "I'm terrible at math." But then she remembered that she had improved her test scores the previous month with extra practice.

Your turn: Write down two negative thoughts and how you would "Catch that Thought."

1. ____

   ____

   ____

2. ____

   ____

   ____

✤ **Turn It Around:** Replace negative thoughts with positive ones. Instead of saying, "I'll never be good at this," try, "With practice, I can get better."

↳ **Check This Out:** Kensley struggled with drawing, but instead of quitting, she told herself, "I am learning, and I will improve."

What is something you are currently learning and want to improve?

____

____

____

____

✤ **Use Positive Affirmations:** Write phrases like "I am smart," "I am kind," or "I am strong."

↳ **Check This Out:** Madison starts her day by reading, "I am smart and can manage any challenge that comes my way"!

Use the sticky notes on the next few pages to write "Positive Affirmation."

I am smart
and can handle
any challenge that
comes my
way!

Practicing Positive Self-Talk

What we say to ourselves matters! Speaking positively to ourselves helps us feel happy and capable.

Try these activities:

* **Positive Self-Talk Cards:** Write down positive statements on index cards and keep them in your backpack or notebook. When you're feeling down, read them for a boost!

  ↳ **Check This Out:** Before a big test, Ramsey pulls out a card that says, "I am prepared, and I will do my best."

* **Encouragement Circle:** With friends or family, take turns saying something positive about each other. This helps everyone feel valued and loved.

Practicing kindness toward others helps you build self-confidence!

  ↳ **Check This Out:** At a sleepover, each girl shares one nice thing about the others. "Raniya is always kind, and Zoe makes us laugh when we need it!"

List positive things you want to say about your friends or family. Don't forget to tell them! LOL

Friend/Family #1

____

____

____

Friend/Family #2

____

____

____

Friend/Family #3

____

____

____

Celebrating Strengths and Accomplishments

"You are awesome, and that's something to celebrate! Take a moment to be proud of the things you do, whether they're big or small."

Here's an activity you can try:

- **Create an 'I Am Amazing' Poster:** Use a big piece of paper to write down all the things you're good at and things you love about yourself. Decorate it with color, glitter, and stickers!

  ↳ **Check This Out:** Leah's poster included "I am a great artist," "I am a good listener," and "I love reading." She used bright colors to draw herself and her friends having a conversation; she added glitter and fun stickers of books to decorate it."

Let's continue celebrating our strengths and accomplishments on the next page...

✽ **Achievement Jar:** Write your achievements on slips of paper and put them in a jar. When you need a confidence boost, pull one out and remember how amazing you are!

↳ **Check This Out:** Emma had a big spelling test coming up, and she was feeling super nervous. She sat on her bed and sighed, thinking, "What if I mess up?" Then she remembered the Achievement Jar she made with her mom during the weekend!

She grabbed the jar, decorated with a ribbon and her name in bubble letters, and opened the lid. Inside were little slips of paper with things she had written down.

She pulled one out and read: "I helped the librarian organize the new books in the library." A smile spread across her face.

Suddenly, that spelling test didn't seem so scary. Emma stood a little taller and told herself, "I've done great things before; I can do this too!"

Embracing Uniqueness and Individuality

"You are one of a kind, and that's something to dance about! Being different is what makes you unique. Here's how to embrace your uniqueness:

❋ **Make a 'What Makes Me Me' List:** Write down things that make you unique, your talents, interests, and personality traits.

⇨ **Example:** "I love drawing comics, I enjoy baking, and I can do back flips!"

'What Makes Me Me' List:

1. ____

2. ____

3. ____

4. ____

5. ____

6. ____

7. ____

8. ____

9. ____

10. ____

❀ **Try a New Hobby:** Explore something you've always been curious about, like painting, writing, dancing, or coding.

↳ **Check This Out:** Amelia always wanted to learn how to knit, so she watched how-to videos and made a scarf!

What are some new hobbies that spark your curiosity?

1. ____
2. ____
3. ____
4. ____
5. ____

↰ Try at least one new hobby within the next couple of weeks.

❀ **Role Model Research:** Learn about inspiring women or girls who embraced their uniqueness and made a change. Think about how you can follow their example in your own way.

Malala Yousafzai is a Pakistani activist who advocates for girls' right to attend school. When she was just 17 years old, she won the Nobel Peace Prize, the youngest person ever to receive it, for her fight for every child's right to education.

↳ **Check This Out:** Learning about Malala Yousafzai inspired Briana to stand up for girls' rights at her school.

Which amazing woman or girl would you like to learn about? Write about someone who stayed true to herself and made a big impact on the world?

Research her and write all about it here:

____

____

____

____

____

Role Model Research continues...

Role Model Research continues...

Now, write about the kind of impact you would like to have on the world.

Final Thought:

Confidence isn't something you find; it's something you build from the inside out! By cheering yourself on, embracing what makes you uniquely YOU, and focusing on your strengths, you're creating a foundation for an amazing, happy, and successful life. So, stand tall, shine bright, and never forget, you are amazing just the way you are! Now go out there and own it!

❀ 2 Making Smart Choices

Hey girl, hi!

Guess what? You're in charge of your story, and every choice you make can shape your outcome! From picking what shoes to wear in the morning to making big decisions about friendships and goals. Learning how to make smart choices is a total game changer. This chapter is about helping you feel confident with your choices, think through your options, and learn from mistakes like a pro. Let's dive in and start making choices that help you shine!

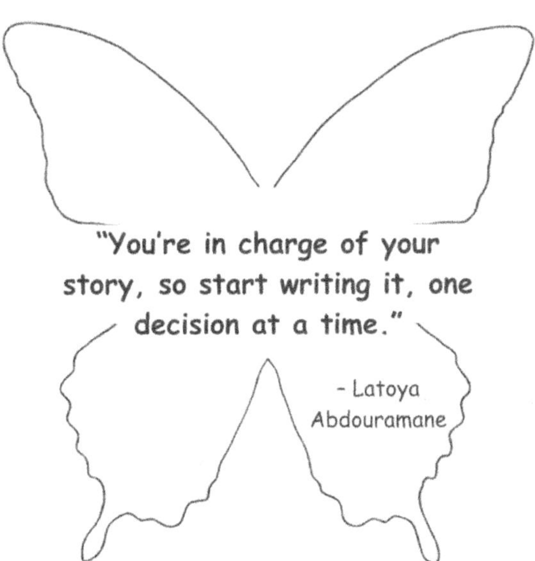

Identifying Options and Considering Consequences

When faced with a decision, it's important to consider the available options and their consequences. Understanding the consequences of each option helps in making the best decision.

* ❋ **The 'What If?' Game:** Think of a decision you need to make and ask, "What if I choose this option? What could happen next?"

* ↳ **Check This Out:** Fatima is deciding whether to finish her homework or watch TV. If she watches TV first, she might run out of time to do her homework. If she finishes her homework first, she can relax without stress.

Let's think about 'possible' consequences for these scenarios:

1. Isabella eats candy every day but only brushes her teeth when she feels like brushing.

Possible Consequence:

____

____

2. Yasmin had to clean her room before she could go to a party, but instead of cleaning, she watched YouTube.

Possible Consequence:

____

____

✾ **Choice Map:** Complete this map, write two decisions one in each wing of the butterfly, and complete the different paths leading to 'possible' consequences.

Think of two opposing choices, like staying up late on a school night or going to sleep on time. One path could show feeling tired the next day, while the path for going to sleep on time could show being well-rested and ready to learn.

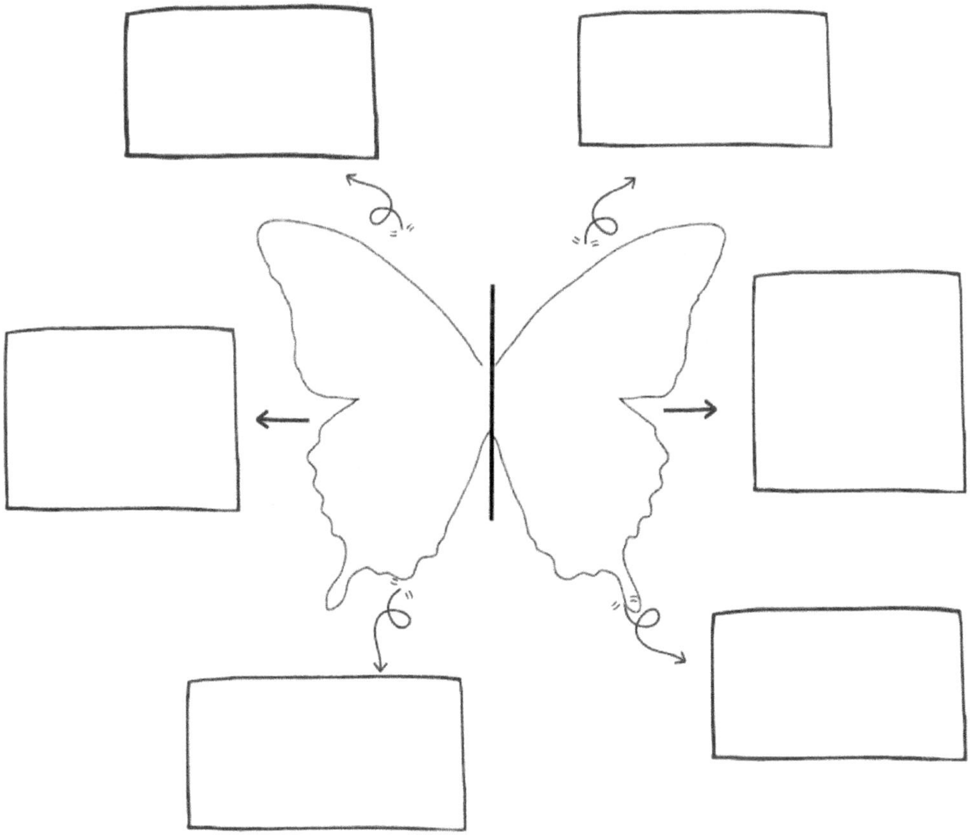

Making Informed Choices

Smart decisions are made by gathering information, thinking about the consequences, and choosing what's best for you.

Have you ever heard of…

* ❃ **The 'Stop, Think, Choose' Method:**

    * ○ **Stop** – Pause before making a quick decision.
    * ○ **Think** – Consider your options and the outcomes.
    * ○ **Choose** – Pick the best choice based on what you know.

    * ↳ **Check This Out:** Brooklyn is looking for a snack before track practice. She sees a few choices: a fruit bowl, Hot Cheetos, and a cupcake with extra frosting. She stops to think and asks herself, "What will make me feel good and give me energy?" After thinking it through, Brooklyn decides to go with the fruit bowl!

* ❃ **Activity: Role-Playing:** Partner up with a friend or family member and act out different decision-making scenarios, like handling a disagreement with a friend or deciding how to spend your allowance.

Learning from Mistakes

Everyone makes mistakes, and that's okay! The key is learning from them so you can make better choices in the future.

* **Mistake Reflection:** When you make a mistake, ask yourself:

  - What happened?
  - What could I do differently next time?
  - What did I learn from this?

↳ **Check This Out:** Sophia forgot her science homework at home. She realized she needed to pack her bag the night before to avoid forgetting important things.

Based on Sophia's mistake:

What happened?

____

What could she do differently next time?

____

What did she learn from this?

____

Final Thought:

Making smart choices is like adding points to your growth board; it takes practice, but each decision helps you grow stronger and wiser! By thinking things through, trusting yourself, and learning from mistakes, you'll build the confidence to handle anything life throws your way. So go ahead, make those choices, and keep shining! You've got this!

❀ 3 Navigating Friendships

Hey girl, hi!

Friendships are wonderful! They bring laughter, fun, and people who have your back. But let's be honest, friendships can also be tricky at times. That's why this chapter is all about helping you manage difficulties like a pro! You'll learn how to choose good friends, stand up for yourself, handle peer pressure, and make choices that feel right for you. Ready to build friendships that lift you up and help you grow? Let's do it!

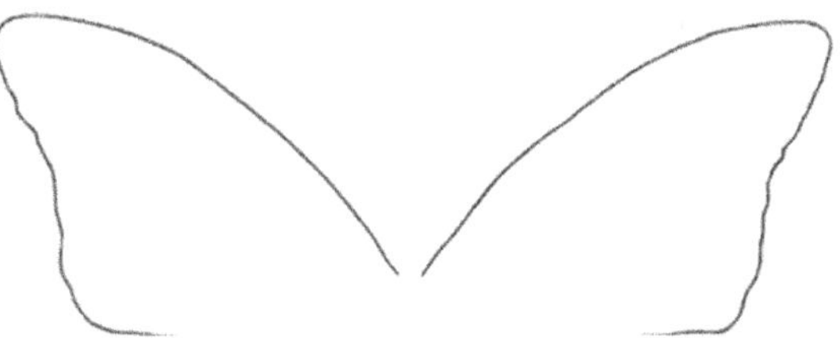

Understanding and Resisting Peer Pressure

Peer pressure happens when friends or classmates try to influence your decisions. Sometimes it can be positive, like encouraging you to try a new hobby, but other times, it can push you into uncomfortable or risky situations.

- **Recognizing Peer Pressure...**

↳ **Check This Out:** Your friends are skipping homeroom class to make dances for YouTube, and they pressure you to do the same. You feel torn because you want to fit in, but you also don't want to get in trouble.

There are three types of peer pressure.

Types of Peer Pressure:

- **Direct** (someone telling you to do something),
- **Indirect** (feeling like you have to do something to fit in), and
- **Self-Imposed** (convincing yourself you have to follow the group).

Dive deeper on the next page!

Direct Peer Pressure:

What to recognize: Someone is trying to make you feel bad or left out if you don't do something.

Friends Say Something Like...
- "Everyone's doing it, don't be the only one who doesn't."
- "If you don't do it, we won't let you hang out with us."
- "Don't be a baby, it's not a big deal."
- "Come on, just try it once!"

> ↳ **Check This Out:** Your friend hands you an energy drink and says, "Everyone is drinking one, come on, just drink it!" Even though you don't like energy drinks, you feel like you have to because your friend is telling you to do it.

Think of a time when someone **directly** pressured you, or a friend, to do something you weren't sure about or didn't want to do? Share what happened and how you or your friend responded.

____

____

____

____

____

Indirect Peer Pressure:

What to recognize: You're doing something only because you want to belong or not be left out.

You Feel Like You Have To...

- Wear clothes just like your friends, even if you don't like them.
- Watch shows or listen to music you don't enjoy just to fit in.
- Laugh at something that's not funny or is mean, because everyone else is.
- Pretend to like something just because your group does.

> ↳ **Check This Out:** At lunch, a group of girls is talking about a new show they all watch. You don't like it, but you pretend to, because you want to be part of the group.

Think of a time when someone **indirectly** pressured you, or a friend, to do something you weren't sure about or didn't want to do? Share what happened and how you or your friend responded.

____

____

____

____

____

Self-Imposed Peer Pressure:

What to recognize: You're putting pressure on yourself to act a certain way, even if no one is saying anything directly.

You Tell Yourself Things Like...
- "If I don't do this, they won't like me."
- "I should just go along with them, so I don't look weird."
- "I don't really want to, but I have to fit in."

> ↳ **Check This Out:** You see that a group of girls at school all wear the same brand of shoes. No one told you to get them, but you start asking your parents for the same shoes, because you think you won't be cool if you don't have them too.

Think of a time when you **pressured yourself** to do something you weren't sure about or didn't want to do? Share what happened.

____

____

____

____

____

✤ Activity: Role-Playing Responses

Practice different ways to respond to peer pressure with a friend or family member. Take turns playing the role of the persuader and the decision-maker.

⇨ **Examples:**
- A friend dares you to say something mean about someone online.
- A group encourages you to lie to your parents.

Discuss different ways to say **no** and stand your ground.

✤ The "No, Thanks" Strategy:

- Keep responses short and confident. **Example:** "No thanks, that's not for me."
- Change the subject. **Example:** "Let's do something else instead."
- Walk away or get help from an adult if needed.

You have Peer Pressure under control!

Assertiveness and Standing Up for Yourself

Being assertive means expressing your thoughts, feelings, and boundaries clearly and respectfully. It helps you maintain healthy friendships and stand up for yourself without being mean or aggressive.

✽ Three Ways to Speak Up:

1. Passive (Keeping quiet when something is not fair)

> ⇨ Example: You're playing a board game during free time at school, and someone skips your turn. You feel upset, but don't say anything and just let it go.

Why it matters: Staying quiet can sometimes make you feel left out or like your feelings don't count.

2. Aggressive (Reacting in a way that hurts feelings)

> ⇨ Example: Someone bumps into you in line, and you shout, "Hey! You're so rude!" and give them a mean look.

Why it matters: Being aggressive can hurt others and make the situation.

3. Assertive (Being brave and kind at the same time)

> ⇨ Example: A friend cuts in front of you during Freeze tag. You take a deep breath and say, "Hey, I was next; let's all take turns so it's fair!"

Why it matters: Being assertive shows that you respect yourself and others; it's like being a kind leader!

❋ **Activity:** Put assertiveness into practice!

↳ **Check This Out:** Kylee's friend makes fun of her handwriting. She feels embarrassed but decides to be assertive. Instead of ignoring it or saying something mean back, she says, "My handwriting will improve, and I'd appreciate it if you didn't make fun of it."

Practice standing tall, maintaining eye contact, and using a firm tone to make your message clear. Doing this in front of a mirror can boost confidence.

↳ **Try saying:** "I don't like that," "Please stop," or "I would rather not."

Making Choices That Align with Personal Values

Your values are the beliefs that guide your decisions and actions. Staying true to them helps you build strong character and meaningful friendships.

❁ **Activity: What Matters to Me?**

Write down five personal values that are important to you in friendships.

⇨ **Examples:** Write things like honesty and respect.

1. ____

2. ____

3. ____

4. ____

5. ____

Think about whether your friendships reflect those values.

↳ **Check This Out:** Gabriel's friends start gossiping about a classmate. Gabriel believes in kindness and doesn't feel right about joining in. Instead of agreeing, she changes the subject after saying, "I don't think we should talk about her like that."

❧ The "True Friend" Test:

Part 1: About Your Friend

Circle the answer that sounds most like your friend!

1. When I am sad, my friend...
   a) Listens and tries to cheer me up
   b) Changes the subject
   c) Laughs or makes fun of me

2. When I make a mistake, my friend...
   a) Forgives me and helps me do better
   b) Gets upset for a long time
   c) Tells everyone what I did

3. When I share good news, my friend...
   a) Is happy and celebrates with me
   b) Does not seem to care
   c) Acts jealously or puts me down

4. When we disagree, my friend...
   a) Talks it out calmly
   b) Stops talking to me for a while
   c) Says mean things or tries to get others on her side

5. When we spend time together, my friend...
   a) Makes me laugh and feel good about myself
   b) Gets bored or distracted
   c) Bosses me around or makes all the choices.

Part 2: About You (because being a 'true friend' goes both ways!)

Check the ones that sound like you!

- ○   I listen when my friends talk to me.
- ○   I say sorry when I've hurt someone's feelings.
- ○   I am happy when my friends succeed.
- ○   I include others and don't leave people out.
- ○   I don't talk behind my friends' backs.

Part 3: Results!

Count how many **A's** you picked in Part 1!

- ○   **4-5 A's:** You've got a 'true friend!' She supports you, respects you, and makes you feel great about being YOU.

- ○   **2-3 A's:** Pretty good friendship! There's love there, but maybe some things to work on, talk, listen, and be kind.

- ○   **0-1 A:** Hmm... time to think. A friend who puts you down or treats you badly may not be a 'true friend.' You deserve respect and kindness!

Final Thought:

Being with your friends should feel like a cozy blanket or a burst of sunshine on a cool day! The best kind of friends cheer you on, laugh with you, and try to get you. Spend time with people who make you feel awesome, say "no thanks" to peer pressure, and stay true to who you are.

So go ahead and stick with the ones who make you smile, dance silly, and feel like your amazing self. You deserve friends who lift you like **butterflies dancing** with the wind!

❀ 4 The Social Media World

Hey girl, hi!

Social media can be fun when chatting with friends, sharing your creativity, and discovering cool new things. But let's be real, it can also come with comparing yourself to others, stressing over likes, or dealing with negativity. No worries, though! In this chapter, we will explore how to make social media fun and positive while protecting your confidence and spreading kindness online.

Ready to scroll with confidence? Follow Me!

Understanding the Impact of Social Media on Self-Esteem and Body Image

Scrolling through social media can sometimes make us feel like everyone else has a perfect life, but what we see online is often just a highlight of the entire picture. Photos are sometimes edited, and people only post their best moments rather than the struggles they face. It's important to remember that social media doesn't always show the full picture.

    ↳ **Check This Out:** Zara sees a friend's vacation photos and feels jealous because her own life seems boring in comparison. Later, she talks to her friend and learns that the trip wasn't as perfect as it appeared; her friend had flight delays and got food poisoning. While Zara wished her friend had a better experience, this helped her realize that social media only shows a part of the story.

❈ **Activity: Reality vs. Social Media**

Look at a picture of someone you **do not know** on social media and think about what might be happening behind the scenes. Discuss with a friend or write down how social media images can be different from real life.

____

____

____

____

____

✾ Affirmation Exercise:

Instead of comparing yourself to others, practice saying positive things about yourself.

Write down five things you like about who you are, beyond just appearance.

1. ______________________________
2. ______________________________
3. ______________________________
4. ______________________________
5. ______________________________

Developing Healthy Social Media Habits

Using social media in a balanced way helps prevent stress and anxiety. Setting limits and focusing on real-life activities can make a 'big' difference in how we feel.

* **Tips for Healthy Social Media Use:**

    - Take a break from screens and spend time doing activities you enjoy (e.g., reading, playing outside, or talking to friends in person).
    - Follow accounts that make you feel happy and inspired rather than ones that make you feel bad about yourself.
    - Think before posting and ask yourself, "Would I say this in person? Does this reflect who I want to be?"

    ↳ **Check This Out:** Nevaeh notices she feels sad every time she checks a certain influencer's page. She decides to unfollow that account and instead follow people who share positive and uplifting content.

* **Activity: Social Media Detox Challenge**

    - Try going one day without checking social media. Instead, work on a craft, read a book, or spend time with family.

    Afterward, reflect on how you felt without it.

Promoting Online Kindness and Responsible Digital Citizenship

Being kind online is just as important as being kind in person. Our words and actions can impact others, even through a screen. Practicing digital kindness helps create a positive social media experience for everyone.

- ✳ The **THINK** Rule Before Posting:
  - ○ Is it **True**?
  - ○ Is it **Helpful**?
  - ○ Is it **Inspiring**?
  - ○ Is it **Necessary**?
  - ○ Is it **Kind**?

- ↳ **Check This Out:** Elizabeth notices a classmate being bullied on social media. Instead of joining in, she leaves a supportive comment and reports the bullying to a trusted adult.

✾ Activity: Online Kindness Chain

Send a kind message, comment, or write a post tagging three people. It can be a compliment, a thank you, or something to brighten their day!

Let's spread kindness online, like icing on a five-layered chocolate cake!

Here are three simple, but sweet **examples** to get you started:

- "I love how you always make people laugh! You're awesome!"
- "Your artwork is so cool! You're super talented!"
- "Thanks for being such a great friend; I'm lucky to know you!"

After You Share:

Take a minute to notice how it feels to make someone smile.

Doesn't spreading positivity feel amazing?

Optional Bonus: Write about how you felt after sending your messages!

____

____

____

____

____

Final Thought:

Social media can be fun, like sharing silly videos, cool pictures, or chatting with friends. But too much of it can feel like brain overload! When you take charge by setting time limits and doing things offline (like dancing, drawing, or playing outside), you'll feel much better. Add a little kindness to your posts and boom, you're spreading good vibes everywhere!

Move like flower petals danceing with the wind!

❀ 5 Managing Your Emotions

Hey girl, hi!

Emotions are like a rollercoaster; they're sometimes exciting, sometimes wild, and sometimes a little overwhelming! But guess what? You have the power to take control. In this chapter, we'll explore how to understand your feelings, handle tough moments like a pro, and find healthy ways to calm down when emotions run high. From dealing with frustration to practicing self-control, you'll learn skills that help you feel strong, confident, and in charge of yourself. Ready to master your emotions? Let's do it!

Identifying and Managing Emotions

Emotions like anger, frustration, and jealousy can be overwhelming, but recognizing them is the first step in handling them in a healthy way.

❋ **Understanding Your Feelings:**

↲ **Check This Out:** Khadijah feels frustrated when her younger sister borrows her things without asking. Instead of yelling, she takes a deep breath and calmly talks about respecting boundaries.

❋ **Activity: Emotion Log** – Write down how you feel when you become upset and what triggered those feelings. This can help to recognize patterns and find better ways to respond.

Start Logging Here…

Date: _________________

How do you feel?

____

What triggered this feeling?

____

Emotion logging continues…

Date: _________________

How do you feel?

____

What triggered this feeling?

____

Date: _________________

How do you feel?

____

What triggered this feeling?

____

Date: _________________

How do you feel?

____

What triggered this feeling?

____

Emotion logging continues...

Date: ___________________

How do you feel?

____

What triggered this feeling?

____

Date: ___________________

How do you feel?

____

What triggered this feeling?

____

Date: ___________________

How do you feel?

____

What triggered this feeling?

____

✿ The Feelings Scale:

Think of your emotions like a thermometer that helps you check in with how you're feeling. Just like the weather, your feelings can be cool, warm, or HOT! Let's break it down:

Cool Zone (Calm & Chill)

You're feeling good, relaxed, and in control. You might be:

- Smiling while playing with friends
- Concentrating on your schoolwork
- Enjoying a quiet moment to yourself

Cool Zone means you're feeling calm and making good choices. This is your **feel-good zone!**

Warm Zone (Getting Heated)

You're starting to feel annoyed, frustrated, or a little upset. You might:

- Feel butterflies in your belly
- Cross your arms and sigh
- Feel like something is bothering you but can't explain why

Warm Zone is your **warning signal** to pause, breathe, and use your cool-down tools before things get too heated!

Hot Zone (Uh-oh, Overheated!)

You're super mad, upset, or out of control. You might:

- Yell, cry, or slam a door
- Say something you don't mean
- Feel like your emotions are too big to handle

Hot Zone means it's time to **cool down right away!** Use your calming strategies (such as deep breathing, counting to 10, squeezing a stress ball, or talking to a trusted adult).

Tip: Check your emotional temperature during the day! Are you cool, warm, or HOT? Knowing where you are helps you manage your feelings like a pro.

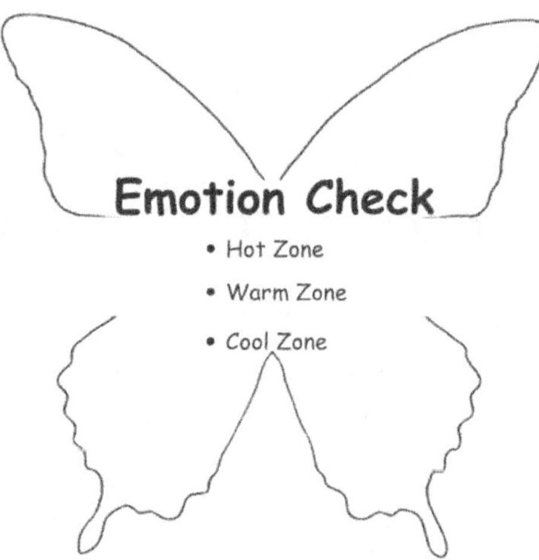

Developing Healthy Coping Mechanisms

When emotions feel too strong, having healthy coping skills can prevent outbursts and help you positively process your feelings.

- ❋ **Coping Strategies:**

    - ○ Deep breathing (inhale for 4 seconds, hold for 4, exhale for 4)
    - ○ Mindfulness (focus on the present moment and what you can control)
    - ○ Physical activity (running, dancing, stretching to release energy)
    - ○ Talking to someone (friend, parent, teacher)
    - ○ Creative outlets (drawing, journaling, listening to positive music)

    - ↳ **Check This Out:** Lyric feels jealous when her best friend spends more time with someone else. Instead of gossiping, she writes in her journal to process her feelings and reminds herself that friendships can grow without losing their value.

- ❋ **Activity: Coping Toolbox**
    - ○ Create a small box filled with items that can help calm emotions (like a stress ball, a favorite quote, or a small notebook for doodling).

Impulse Control and Resisting Negative Urges

Sometimes, we react too quickly without thinking, which can lead to regret. Let's **stop** and **think** before acting. This is a valuable skill.

❀ **Pause Before Reacting:**

- Count to 10 before speaking or acting when feeling upset.
- Ask yourself, "How will I feel about this decision later?"
- Use "I" statements instead of blaming. **Example:** "I feel hurt when you ignore me," instead of "You're so mean."

↳ **Check This Out:** Marley is tempted to send a mean text to her friend after an argument. Instead, she waits until she cools down, then writes her thoughts in a notebook first. Later, she talks it out in person and resolves the issue calmly.

❀ **Activity: The Stop-Think-Act Game**
- Have someone give different situations (e.g., "A friend takes your seat," "Someone teases you"). Practice stopping, thinking, and then acting calmly.

Making Mindful Choices in Words and Actions

The way we respond to emotions affects our relationships and self-confidence. Choosing words and actions carefully leads to better outcomes.

- ❋ **The Power of Words:**

    - ○ Words can help or hurt, so always choose kindness.
    - ○ Before speaking, ask: **Is it true? Is it kind? Is it necessary?**

    - ↳ **Check This Out:** Kellie is about to say something unkind in frustration, but remembers the STOP, THINK and then ACT rule. She chooses to take a deep breath and speak calmly instead.

- ❋ **Activity: Mindful Compliments**
    - ○ Practice giving genuine compliments instead of focusing on negativity. This helps train the brain to think positively even in tough situations.

- ⇨ **Example:**
  Instead of saying, "I can't believe she wore that," try saying, "I love how confident she is in her style!"

By practicing kind thoughts like this, you train your brain to look for the good in others, and in yourself, even when things feel challenging.

Final Thought:

Emotions are powerful, but you can control how you respond to them. By recognizing your feelings, using healthy coping strategies, practicing self-control, and choosing kindness, you can navigate life's challenges with confidence!

❀ 6 The Power of Words

Hey girl, hi!

Your words are powerful! They can lift people up, spread kindness, and help you express yourself with confidence. But let's be real, sometimes, communication can be tricky, especially when dealing with disagreements or tough conversations. No worries, though! In this chapter, you'll dive into fun ways to build strong friendships, handle conflict like a leader, and speak up for yourself while staying kind and respectful.

Ready to use your voice to make the world a more positive place? Let's do it!

Active Listening and Communication Skills

Listening is just as important as speaking in communication. Active listening means fully focusing on the person talking, understanding their message, and responding thoughtfully.

❋ **Keys to Active Listening:**

- Maintain eye contact to show engagement.
- Nod or respond with short phrases like "I understand" or "That makes sense."
- Avoid interrupting and let the person finish speaking before responding.
- Summarize what was said to ensure understanding (e.g., "So you're saying you felt left out when we didn't invite you?").

↳ **Check This Out:** Harper's friend, Natalia, is upset because she wasn't invited to a sleepover. Instead of dismissing her feelings, Harper listens carefully, acknowledges Natalia's feelings, and reassures her that their friendship is important.

✻ Activity: Partner Listening Exercise

- Pair up and take turns talking about a favorite hobby or experience. The listener must repeat back what they heard before switching roles. This helps develop strong listening skills.

➩ **Example:** Amyrah and Gricelda pair up. Amyrah goes first and says, "My favorite hobby is painting. I love using bright colors and making pictures of flowers."

Gricelda listens carefully and then repeats back: "Your favorite hobby is painting, and you like using bright colors to make flower pictures."

Then they switch, and Gricelda shares her favorite activity while Amyrah listens and repeats what she heard. This helps both girls become better listeners and feel listened to.

Empathy and Perspective-Taking

Empathy means understanding and sharing others' feelings. Putting yourself in someone else's shoes can help you respond with kindness and build a deeper connection.

❊ **Ways to Show Empathy:**

- Pay attention to others' emotions, notice their body language, and tone of voice.
- Imagine how you would feel in their situation.
- Respond with kindness and understanding rather than judgment.

↳ **Check This Out:** Naomi sees a classmate sitting alone at lunch. Instead of ignoring her, Naomi remembers a time when she felt lonely and decided to invite her classmate to sit with her.

✾ Activity: Perspective Swap

- Write or act out a situation from another person's point of view. How might they be feeling? How would you want to be treated if you were in their place?

  ➪ **Example:** Think back to Naomi from the last page. She remembered a time she felt lonely, so she invited her classmate, because she would want someone to invite her.

  ↴ **Your turn...**

Conflict Resolution Strategies

Conflicts are a natural part of relationships; handling them with respect can turn disagreements into learning experiences.

- ❋ **Steps for Resolving Conflicts:**

    - ○ **Stay Calm:** Take deep breaths before reacting.
    - ○ **Listen to the Other Person:** Try to understand their perspective.
    - ○ **Express Yourself Clearly:** Use "I" statements like "I feel upset when…" instead of blaming.
    - ○ **Find a Solution Together:** Be willing to compromise and find a fair resolution.
    - ○ **Apologize When Needed:** Saying sorry shows maturity and helps rebuild trust.

    - ↳ **Check This Out:** Kennedi and her friend argue over who gets to pick the game at recess. Instead of yelling, Kennedi suggests they take turns. They both agree, and the problem is solved.

- ❋ **Activity: Role-Playing Conflict Resolution**
    - ○ Act out common disagreements (e.g., borrowing items without asking, interrupting during a conversation) and practice using negotiation, compromise, and apologies to resolve them.

Assertiveness and Expressing Needs and Opinions Respectfully

Being assertive means speaking up for yourself while still being respectful. It's different from being passive (not speaking up at all) or aggressive (being rude or forceful).

❊ **Tips for Being Assertive:**

- Stand tall and use a confident voice.
- Use "I" statements instead of accusing others.
- Stay calm and polite, even when disagreeing.
- Set boundaries and say "no" when needed without feeling guilty.

↳ **Check This Out:** Willow's friends pressured her to join in on a prank, but she knows it's wrong. She calmly says, "I don't think that's a good idea. I don't want to get in trouble."

What is another way Willow could say "NO" with confidence?

____

____

✽ Activity: Assertive Communication Practice

Check out these three situations. Write down ways you can express your needs and opinions respectfully. Practice writing your response in a strong, respectful voice.

Situation 1: You're at a sleepover, and your friend wants to order pizza with spicy peppers, but you don't like spicy food.

____

____

Situation 2: You're working on a group project, but one classmate is making all the decisions and not allowing anyone else to share ideas.

____

____

Situation 3: Your classmate borrows your favorite markers every day without asking.

____

____

↰ These scenarios will help you learn that being assertive means using your voice in a kind, clear, and confident way, so everyone feels heard and respected!

⇨ **Examples** of 'possible' responses:

Assertive Response Situation 1: You smile and say, "Hey, spicy food hurts my stomach. Can we get half of the pizza with something milder like cheese or pepperoni?"

Assertive Response Situation 2: You say, "Hey, we all have good ideas. Can I share mine, too? So, we can work together better."

Assertive Response Situation 3: You say, "I'm happy to share sometimes, but I need to use my markers too. Please ask me first next time."

Final Thought:

The way we communicate shapes our relationships and self-confidence. By listening actively, showing empathy, resolving conflicts peacefully, and speaking assertively, you can create a positive impact in your interactions with others. Words are powerful; use them wisely!

❀ Conclusion: You've Got This, Girl!

Wow, look at all the amazing things you've learned! From cheering yourself on with positive self-talk to making smart choices, building strong friendships, and handling tough emotions, you've built a powerful toolbox of confidence, kindness, and courage.

You've discovered how to shine by celebrating what makes you 'YOU,' how to speak up for yourself respectfully, and how to stay true to your values, even when it's not easy. You've explored how to use social media in a healthy way, practiced being a great friend and listener, and learned how to turn big feelings into smart actions.

Remember, your voice matters, your choices matter, and YOU matter. Keep using the skills you've learned, continue being kind to yourself and others, and never forget you're brave, brilliant, and unstoppable.

Now go out there and shine because the world needs girls like you!

NOTES

NOTES

NOTES

❀ References

1. Highlighting Positive Qualities

American Academy of Pediatrics. (2022). Helping children develop healthy self-esteem. VIA Institute on Character. (n.d.). Strengths & children/schools

2. Making Smart Choices

Child Mind Institute. (n.d.). Helping kids make decisions Kids Health. (n.d.). How to make good decisions.

3. Navigating Friendships

American Psychological Association. (2023). How to help kids navigate friendships and peer relationships Nemours Kids Health. (n.d.). Making friends.

4. The Social Media World

American Academy of Child & Adolescent Psychiatry. (2024). Social media and teens Common Sense Media. (n.d.). Social media tips for kids and tweens.

5. Managing Your Emotions

American Psychological Association. (n.d.). How to help kids understand and manage their emotions PBS KIDS for Parents. (n.d.). Managing emotions

6. The Power of Words

Edutopia. (2018). Showing students the power of words Understood.org. (2023). How positive language can help kids.

❀ Acknowledgements

It has always been a dream of mine to publish a book that helps girls and mothers to reclaim their power.

I am deeply grateful to every teacher with whom I have built relationships over the years for recognizing the importance of this project and encouraging me along the way.

Many thanks to my friends for allowing me to speak endlessly about my work, even as time passed, always reassuring me that I am capable of wonderful things and holding me accountable when it came time to follow through on my plans.

Most importantly, my greatest thanks go to all the girls who will use this workbook to grow in their confidence, and to the mothers who will become better supporters because of it.

I appreciate all of you!

✽ About the Author

LATOYA ABDOURAMANE is a mother, writer, educator, registered social worker, and mentor with a deep commitment to education, youth development, and community service. Originally from New Orleans, she now resides in the Acadiana region of South-Central Louisiana, where she continues to pour her passion into teaching and mentoring. Latoya currently serves as an eighth-grade teacher, working to inspire critical thinking, confidence, and academic growth in her students.

Beyond the classroom, she is passionate about mentoring young girls, helping them develop strong identities, leadership skills, and a belief in their potential. As a writer, Latoya uses her voice to explore meaningful themes rooted in culture, growth, and lived experience. In her personal life, she enjoys reading, lifelong learning, and spending quality time with her son, Asim, often building imaginative LEGO creations together. Her work and interests reflect her belief in creativity, education, and connection.

9 7 9 8 9 9 9 4 4 4 1 6 0 2